scan to leave a review:

Product designed and published by:

KIKI
Potter

Congratulation!

MAY YOUR BABY BE BLESSED WITH
GOOD HEALTH, LOVE AND
LAUGHTER

Waiting for Baby!

ADVICE, WISHES, AND MEMORIES
ON YOUR BABY SHOWER

name: ⟡ . . . . ⟡

date: ⟡ . . . . ⟡

place: ⟡ . . . . ⟡

In celebration of:

BABY
Shower

From: ....

E-mail: ....

Advice for parents:

....
....
....

Wishes for baby:

....
....
....

From: ....

E-mail: ....

BABY
Shower

Advice for parents:

....

....

....

Wishes for baby:

....

....

....

BABY
Shower

From: ....

E-mail: ....

Advice for parents:

◇...◇

◇...◇

◇...◇

Wishes for baby:

◇...◇

◇...◇

◇...◇

From: ....

E-mail: ....

BABY
Shower

Advice for parents:

◇..◇

◇..◇

◇..◇

Wishes for baby:

◇..◇

◇..◇

◇..◇

BABY
Shower

From: ....

E-mail: ....

Advice for parents:

....

....

....

Wishes for baby:

....

....

....

From: ....

E-mail: ....

BABY
Shower

Advice for parents:

....

....

....

Wishes for baby:

....

....

....

BABY
Shower

From: ....

E-mail: ....

Advice for parents:

....

....

....

Wishes for baby:

....

....

....

From: ....

E-mail: ....

BABY
Shower

Advice for parents:

....

....

....

Wishes for baby:

....

....

....

BABY
Shower

From: ....

E-mail: ....

Advice for parents:

....

....

....

Wishes for baby:

....

....

....

From: ....

E-mail: ....

BABY

Shower

Advice for parents:

◇..◇

◇..◇

◇..◇

Wishes for baby:

◇..◇

◇..◇

◇..◇

BABY
Shower

From: ....

E-mail: ....

Advice for parents:

....

....

....

Wishes for baby:

....

....

....

From: ....

E-mail: ....

BABY

Shower

Advice for parents:

....

....

....

Wishes for baby:

....

....

....

BABY
Shower

From: ....

E-mail: ....

Advice for parents:

....

....

....

Wishes for baby:

....

....

....

From: ....

E-mail: ....

BABY

Shower

Advice for parents:

◇ .... ◇

◇ .... ◇

◇ .... ◇

Wishes for baby:

◇ .... ◇

◇ .... ◇

◇ .... ◇

BABY
Shower

From: ....

E-mail: ....

Advice for parents:

◇ .... ◇

◇ .... ◇

◇ .... ◇

Wishes for baby:

◇ .... ◇

◇ .... ◇

◇ .... ◇

From: ....

E-mail: ....

BABY
Shower

Advice for parents:

....

....

....

Wishes for baby:

....

....

....

BABY
Shower

From: ....

E-mail: ....

Advice for parents:

....

....

....

Wishes for baby:

....

....

....

From: ....

E-mail: ....

BABY
Shower

Advice for parents:

....
....
....

Wishes for baby:

....
....
....

BABY
Shower

From: ....

E-mail: ....

Advice for parents:

....

....

....

Wishes for baby:

....

....

....

From: ....

E-mail: ....

BABY
Shower

Advice for parents:

....

....

....

Wishes for baby:

....

....

....

BABY
Shower

From: ....

E-mail: ....

Advice for parents:

....

....

....

Wishes for baby:

....

....

....

From: ....

E-mail: ....

BABY
Shower

Advice for parents:

....

....

....

Wishes for baby:

....

....

....

BABY
Shower

From: ....

E-mail: ....

Advice for parents:

◇ .... ◇

◇ .... ◇

◇ .... ◇

Wishes for baby:

◇ .... ◇

◇ .... ◇

◇ .... ◇

From: ....

E-mail: ....

BABY
Shower

Advice for parents:

....

....

....

Wishes for baby:

....

....

....

BABY
Shower

From: ....

E-mail: ....

Advice for parents:

◇ .... ◇

◇ .... ◇

◇ .... ◇

Wishes for baby:

◇ .... ◇

◇ .... ◇

◇ .... ◇

From: ....

E-mail: ....

BABY
Shower

Advice for parents:

◇...◇

◇...◇

◇...◇

Wishes for baby:

◇...◇

◇...◇

◇...◇

BABY
Shower

From: ....

E-mail: ....

Advice for parents:

....

....

....

Wishes for baby:

....

....

....

From: ....

E-mail: ....

BABY
Shower

Advice for parents:

....
....
....

Wishes for baby:

....
....
....

BABY Shower

From: ....

E-mail: ....

Advice for parents:

....

....

....

Wishes for baby:

....

....

....

From: ....

E-mail: ....

BABY
Shower

Advice for parents:

◇ .... ◇

◇ .... ◇

◇ .... ◇

Wishes for baby:

◇ .... ◇

◇ .... ◇

◇ .... ◇

BABY
Shower

From: ....

E-mail: ....

Advice for parents:

....

....

....

Wishes for baby:

....

....

....

From: ....

E-mail: ....

BABY
Shower

Advice for parents:

....

....

....

Wishes for baby:

....

....

....

BABY Shower

From: ....

E-mail: ....

Advice for parents:

....

....

....

Wishes for baby:

....

....

....

From: ....

E-mail: ....

BABY
Shower

Advice for parents:

◇...◇

◇...◇

◇...◇

Wishes for baby:

◇...◇

◇...◇

◇...◇

BABY Shower

From: ....

E-mail: ....

Advice for parents:

◇ .... ◇

◇ .... ◇

◇ .... ◇

Wishes for baby:

◇ .... ◇

◇ .... ◇

◇ .... ◇

From: ....

E-mail: ....

BABY

Shower

Advice for parents:

....

....

....

Wishes for baby:

....

....

....

BABY
Shower

From: ....

E-mail: ....

Advice for parents:

◇ .... ◇

◇ .... ◇

◇ .... ◇

Wishes for baby:

◇ .... ◇

◇ .... ◇

◇ .... ◇

From: ....

E-mail: ....

BABY
Shower

Advice for parents:

....

....

....

Wishes for baby:

....

....

....

BABY Shower

From: ....

E-mail: ....

Advice for parents:

....

....

....

Wishes for baby:

....

....

....

From: ....

E-mail: ....

BABY
Shower

Advice for parents:

....

....

....

Wishes for baby:

....

....

....

BABY
Shower

From: ....

E-mail: ....

Advice for parents:

◇ ·· ◇

◇ ·· ◇

◇ ·· ◇

Wishes for baby:

◇ ·· ◇

◇ ·· ◇

◇ ·· ◇

From: ....

E-mail: ....

BABY
Shower

Advice for parents:

....

....

....

Wishes for baby:

....

....

....

BABY
Shower

From: ....

E-mail: ....

Advice for parents:

....

....

....

Wishes for baby:

....

....

....

From: ....

E-mail: ....

BABY
Shower

Advice for parents:

....

....

....

Wishes for baby:

....

....

....

BABY

Shower

From: ....

E-mail: ....

Advice for parents:

....

....

....

Wishes for baby:

....

....

....

From: ....

E-mail: ....

BABY
Shower

Advice for parents:

....

....

....

Wishes for baby:

....

....

....

BABY
Shower

From: ....

E-mail: ....

Advice for parents:

....

....

....

Wishes for baby:

....

....

....

From: ....

E-mail: ....

BABY
Shower

Advice for parents:

....

....

....

Wishes for baby:

....

....

....

BABY
Shower

From: ....

E-mail: ....

Advice for parents:

....

....

....

Wishes for baby:

....

....

....

From: ....

E-mail: ....

BABY
Shower

Advice for parents:

....

....

....

Wishes for baby:

....

....

....

BABY
Shower

From: ....

E-mail: ....

Advice for parents:

....

....

....

Wishes for baby:

....

....

....

From: ....

E-mail: ....

BABY
Shower

Advice for parents:

⋄................................⋄

⋄................................⋄

⋄................................⋄

Wishes for baby:

⋄................................⋄

⋄................................⋄

⋄................................⋄

BABY
Shower

From: ....

E-mail: ....

Advice for parents:

....

....

....

Wishes for baby:

....

....

....

From: ....

E-mail: ....

BABY

Shower

Advice for parents:

◇..◇

◇..◇

◇..◇

Wishes for baby:

◇..◇

◇..◇

◇..◇

BABY
Shower

From: ....

E-mail: ....

Advice for parents:

....

....

....

Wishes for baby:

....

....

....

From: ....

E-mail: ....

BABY
Shower

Advice for parents:

....
....
....

Wishes for baby:

....
....
....

Gift Tracker

GIFT
Tracker

THANK YOU EMAIL SENT	Gift received:	Given by:
◯		
◯		
◯		
◯		
◯		
◯		
◯		
◯		

GIFT
Tracker

Gift received:	Given by:	THANK YOU EMAIL SENT
		◯
		◯
		◯
		◯
		◯
		◯
		◯
		◯

GIFT  Tracker

THANK YOU EMAIL SENT	Gift received:	Given by:
◯		
◯		
◯		
◯		
◯		
◯		
◯		
◯		

GIFT
Tracker

Gift received:

Given by:

○

○

○

○

○

○

○

○

GIFT  Tracker

THANK YOU EMAIL SENT	Gift received:	Given by:
◯		
◯		
◯		
◯		
◯		
◯		
◯		
◯		

Gift received:

Given by:

THANK YOU
EMAIL SENT

○

○

○

○

○

○

○

○

GIFT Tracker

THANK YOU EMAIL SENT	Gift received:	Given by:
◯		
◯		
◯		
◯		
◯		
◯		
◯		
◯		

GIFT
Tracker

Gift received:	Given by:	THANK YOU EMAIL SENT
....	....	◯
....	....	◯
....	....	◯
....	....	◯
....	....	◯
....	....	◯
....	....	◯
....	....	◯

GIFT
Tracker

THANK YOU EMAIL SENT	Gift received:	Given by:
◯		
◯		
◯		
◯		
◯		
◯		
◯		
◯		

GIFT
Tracker

Gift received:	Given by:	THANK YOU EMAIL SENT
....	....	◯
....	....	◯
....	....	◯
....	....	◯
....	....	◯
....	....	◯
....	....	◯
....	....	◯

Memories

Plans, notes

PLANS, Notes

PLANS,
Notes

PLANS,

Notes

PLANS,
Notes

PLANS,
Notes

PLANS,
Notes

PLANS,

Notes

PLANS,
Notes

PLANS,

Notes

PLANS.

Notes

PLANS,
Notes

PLANS,
Notes

PLANS,
Notes

Printed in Great Britain
by Amazon